D1320732

TALK ABOUT
Racism

Cath Senker

WAYLAND

First published in 2008 by Wayland

Copyright © Wayland 2008

Wayland
338 Euston Road
London NW1 3BH

Wayland Australia
Level 17/207 Kent Street
Sydney, NSW 2000

Editor: Camilla Lloyd
Consultant: Jayne Wright
Designer: Tim Mayer
Picture researcher: Kathy Lockley
Map: Ian Thompson

Picture Acknowledgments: The author and publisher would like to thank the following for allowing their pictures to be reproduced in this publication: Cover photograph: Zave Smith/Jupiter Images. Andrew Holbrooke/Corbis: 1, 13; Benjamin Lowy/Corbis: 21; Bettman/Corbis: 9; CTK Czech News Agency/CTK/PA Photos: 14, 20BR, 25TR, 27TL, 30TR, 32TR, 36TL, 39TR, 42TR; David H. Wells/Corbis: 32; Ed Kashi/Corbis: 16; Eric Gay/AP/PA Photos: 27; Haydn West/PA Archive/PA Photos: 22; Howard Davies/Corbis: 36; Howard Davies/repordigital.co.uk: 37; Hulton Archive/Getty Images: 6; Images Source/Corbis: 4; Jacky Chapman/Photofusion: 31; Jed Leicester/Corbis: 45; John Birdsall Social Issues Photo Library: 17; Judy Harrison/Photofusion: 33; Martial Trezzini/AP/PA Photos: 28; Martin Meissner/AP/PA Photos: 20; Nancy Ney/Corbis: 40-41; Neville Elder/Corbis: 25; Nicholas Bailey/Rex Features: 35; Paul Dymond/Alamy: 8; Peter Dench/Corbis: 10-11; Ralf-Finn Hestoft: 15; Reuters/Corbis: 5; Richard Levine/Alamy: 29; Ruben Sprich/Reuters/Corbis: 26; Sam Diephuis/zefa/Corbis: 38; Thierry Orban/Corbis Sygma: 12; Ullstein/Topfoto/Topfoto.co.uk: 30; Ulrike Preuss/Photofusion: 18-19; Will & Deni McIntyre/ Corbis: 42; Yoav Lemmer/POOL /epa/Corbis: 44; Yves Logghe/AP/PA Photos: 23; Zave Smith/ Jupiter Images: 43.

Acknowledgments:
The author would like to thank the following for permission to reproduce material in this book: p.5 Quote from *Preventing and Addressing Racism in Schools*, London Borough of Ealing, UK, 2003; p.7 Quote from *The Farmworker's Daughter* by Rose Castillo Guilbault; p.11 In the Media from *The Australian*, 27 October 2006; p.13 'Terrorist Gangs' from Americans for Legal Immigration website; p.14 Mrs Zupková's story by Laura Cashman; p.21 Facts from Unite Against Fascism, UK; p.24 Facts from Human Rights and Equal Opportunity Commission, Australia; p.29 In the media from a feature about an anti-Semitic attack on a 12-year-old by David Cohen, *Evening Standard*, 27 September 2006; p. 31 Quote from 'Family: Southside Schoolteacher Discriminates Against Muslim Girl' May 31, 2006 © 2007 by News4Jax.com; p.32 From the Findings 'Children's perspectives on believing and belonging' published in 2005 by the Joseph Rowntree Foundation. Reproduced by permission of the Joseph Rowntree Foundation; p.38 Mahmood's story from 'Young Voices - Mahmood,' UNHCR, Australia; p.41 Action points from 'We are experts – what young people want,' Teachernet, UK; p.43 Action points from ChildLine, UK.

British Library Cataloguing in Publication Data:
Senker, Cath
   Talk about racism
   1. Racism - Juvenile literature
   I. Title II. Racism
   305.8

ISBN: 978 0 7502 4935 5

Printed in China

Wayland is a division of Hachette Children's Books, an Hachette Livre UK company

CONTENTS

Chapter 1
What is racism? 4

Chapter 2
Why are people racist? 10

Chapter 3
What do racists do? 16

Chapter 4
Hidden racism 24

Chapter 5
What is religious prejudice? 28

Chapter 6
Racism against migrants 34

Chapter 7
What can we do about racism? 40

Glossary 46

Further information 47

Index 48

Chapter 1

What is racism?

People in society are all different. Some of us are tall and some are short, and our skin and hair colour vary. We have different ideas and we enjoy doing different things. Some people make judgements about people just because of how they look or behave, without even getting to know them. This is called prejudice.

For example, schoolchildren may look at another child in a wheelchair and think he is not very clever or good at his schoolwork because he is disabled. However, he might be a mathematics genius; it just happens that he cannot walk very well.

It is common for black and ethnic minority children to experience racism at school.

Some people are prejudiced against others who have a different skin colour or are from a different ethnic group or culture. They feel superior to them. This is racism.

Racism exists in many forms. For instance, in a classroom where most of the children are white, they might bully the few black children. People who are racist and have power in society can act against a whole group. An example of this happened in South Africa until 1990. Up until then a small number of white people ruled over a majority of black people. The government kept people of different races apart. White people were provided with far better homes, schools and hospitals than black people.

These extreme right-wing Hindus in Bhopal, central India, are protesting against an attack by Muslims. In the early 2000s, there were serious outbreaks of racial tension between Hindus and Muslims in India.

Racism around the world

Racism exists in most societies. In the USA, for instance, there is racism among white people against Hispanics, African-Americans and Asians. It is not just white people who can be racist. In India, extreme right-wing Hindus believe that Hindus are superior to Muslims (who make up about one-fifth of the population). They say that India should be for the Hindu majority and are racist towards Muslims. Racism is an international problem, and it has a long history.

It happened to me

'When I was in the juniors [primary school] they used to call me names in the playground all the time, like "nigger". They used to upset me and sometimes I would get so mad I would fight and then I would get in trouble. I was always the one who got in trouble. They didn't do nothing to the ones that was doing it.'

Child growing up in London in the early 2000s.

Where does racism come from?

Throughout history, there have been different kinds of prejudice. Sometimes, people did not trust others from abroad or people who had a different lifestyle. For example, the Roma (or gypsies) are travelling people who move from place to place. They left India in about the 10th century CE and moved around Europe. The groups who were already settled in Europe generally distrusted the gypsies and thought they were criminals.

European empires

A new form of prejudice arose between the 16th and the 19th centuries, when European countries took over large parts of the Caribbean, the Americas, Asia and Africa. They ruled them as their colonies. In the Caribbean and the Americas, most of the indigenous population were killed, or died from disease. The European colonists needed to find other workers for their farms. They seized millions of Africans and bought them as slaves.

As rulers of the colonies, the white Europeans came to believe that they were superior to the black Africans they had enslaved and the other non-white people they ruled over. The idea of racism based on skin colour developed. It grew strong as the European empires reached their height in the 19th century and continued to rule their colonies in the following century.

Mass migration

After World War II ended in 1945, most colonies became free of their European rulers but had been left desperately poor. At the time, European countries needed to rebuild their economies after the war.

Police in London search a young black man in Notting Hill, London, after riots in 1958. Young white gangs who were hostile to the African-Caribbean immigrants had attacked their community.

The world in 1900

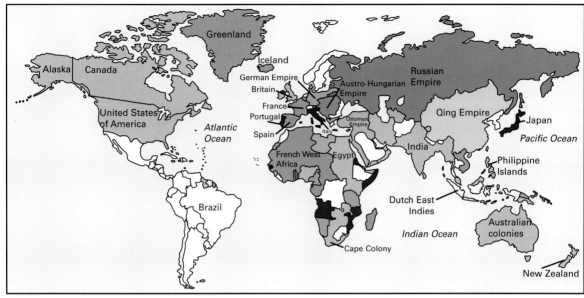

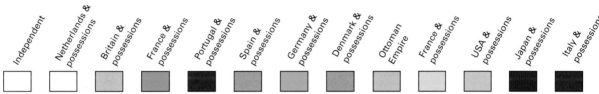

European countries invited the people of their former colonies in Africa, Asia and the Caribbean to come to work in Europe. Although they were greatly needed, these new workers faced racism when they arrived. Many local people thought they were inferior and did not accept their different customs. In general, the newcomers were offered the dirtiest, most dangerous and the lowest-paid jobs.

As in Europe, from the 1960s, the USA, Canada and Australia changed their immigration policies to allow people from around the world to enter, rather than just Europeans as before. These countries provided good job opportunities for immigrants (people who migrated and settled). However, non-European immigrants often came up against racism in their new homeland.

In many Western countries (the countries of the Western world, especially Europe and North America) laws were introduced from the 1970s to make racism illegal, but prejudice is deep-seated and often rooted in people's upbringing, so racism is still with us today.

In 1900, large numbers of Western countries had a foreign empire. Britain had the largest empire, with colonies in many areas of the world.

Racism against migrants

Today there is still racism, particularly against refugees and migrants. People become refugees when they flee their own land because of persecution, and attempt to seek safety in another land. People who move to another part of their own country, or to another land, are called migrants. Many international migrants (migrants from other countries) stay for a while to work and return home afterwards. Some decide to remain in their new homeland. They then become known as immigrants. The prejudice against them is not just to do with skin colour, although this is usually a factor. It is because they have a different culture too, and are often seen as outsiders.

This female Asian immigrant is a banana worker in Tully, Queensland, Australia.

For example, some people in Western Europe have racist attitudes not only towards black and Asian immigrants but also towards eastern Europeans who have come to work – even though they are white.

It happened to me

'When I was five, mum took me from Nogales in Mexico (by the border with the USA) to live on an isolated farm in California. Mum spent her life on the farm and never even learnt English properly. My stepdad was poor and uneducated. He worked as a farm labourer for low wages. If you were young and Mexican it was understood you would work in the fields ... My first time was when I was eleven. But I wanted to go to college and have a good career. Eventually I succeeded and became a journalist.'

Rose Castillo Guilbault, growing up as a Mexican immigrant in the 1960s, found that Mexicans were expected to be farmworkers.

Many forms of racism

Racism can evolve in different circumstances. It is not always a matter of white prejudice against black people. Another example of racism comes from Israel, a country of many races. Since its formation in 1948, there has been conflict between Israelis and the Palestinians, who lost their country when Israel was formed. Many Israelis have racist attitudes towards Palestinians, believing they are violent and hostile and that it is not possible to live with them in peace. In turn, many Arabs who sympathize with the Palestinians have racist views of Israelis too. Racism can take many forms depending on where you are, the history of the country, and what is going on around you.

Migrant Mexican workers pick strawberries in California, USA, in 1963. By 2004, one in every three workers in farming, fishing and forestry in the USA was Mexican.

Chapter 2

Why are people racist?

No one is born racist, and racists can come from any type of background. There are many reasons why people might develop prejudices. Some people might follow role models who are racist. Perhaps their parents or school friends are prejudiced. Some young people join gangs. If most of the members are racist, then a new member may feel the need to adopt the same attitude.

Ignorance can be a cause of racism too. If people have never met individuals from other cultures and do not understand their customs, they may develop prejudices against them because they are different. They may hear certain fixed views, and believe them because they do not know any better.

Stereotypes

A stereotype is an idea of a particular type of person or thing. This idea is so widely used that, for many people, it has become fixed as 'true', even though it may not necessarily be so. Stereotypes feature regularly in the media. For instance, some elements of the Western media can be accused of sometimes showing Muslims as people who follow a very strict and aggressive religion that supports terrorism, and who want to keep separate from wider society. Yet the majority of Muslims are not like this. This is a negative stereotype, which is damaging and encourages racism.

People often make judgements about others without getting to know them. Many non-Muslims hold stereotyped views of Muslim women who cover up in public.

Blaming others

People may believe in stereotypes and hold racist attitudes but not act upon them. Others take action on the streets. They may join racist organizations, even if they are illegal. For example, in Russia since the 1990s many skinhead groups have sprung up. They have neo-Nazi views, meaning that they follow Adolf Hitler's racist Nazi ideas that were developed in the 1930s. The skinheads believe in a 'pure' Russian race and hate people from other countries and cultures.

Neo-Nazi skinheads are usually secondary school students, vocational students (learning a trade or skill) or young unemployed people. How do they become racist? Experts believe the skinhead groups have grown because of the economic crisis in Russia and the upheaval in society after the collapse of the Soviet Union in 1990. The young neo-Nazis blame immigrants for the difficulties in their society.

In the
media

'You hear more and more stories of treatment of the Islamic community that really is substandard by members of our own wider community. It is vilification [describing them harshly and unfairly], picking them out of the crowd because they dress differently or they speak differently. If we are not careful we risk raising a generation of Australians who will have a bias against Islam.'

Australian Federal Police Commissioner Mick Keelty believes the media is responsible for fuelling racist attitudes against Australian Muslims.

Scapegoating

Often when a country is in crisis, people look for others to blame. This is called scapegoating – blaming a group of people for problems that they didn't cause. It is an important cause of racism.

Far-right organizations, such as the neo-Nazis in Russia, tend to scapegoat immigrants and claim that if they left the country, the difficulties would go away. In the USA too, far-right groups say that Mexican migrants are responsible for the increase in violent crime and even that they are terrorists. In fact, a 2005 study found that increased immigration led to a reduction in the crime rate. Immigrants were less likely to commit crime than Americans. They are simply being scapegoated.

At this demonstration in Paris, France, young Muslims protest for their right to wear Islamic dress, including the hijab (a headscarf worn by Muslim women and girls).

A border guard arrests a Mexican man who has entered the USA illegally. Mexicans are often scapegoated for problems in the USA but their work is vital to the economy.

Cultural differences

Rather than being openly racist against immigrants, some say it is impossible for people from different backgrounds to live together peacefully because of their cultural differences. For instance, France is a secular (non-religious) country by law. Many French citizens feel that religious people coming into the country – mainly Muslims – are destroying the secular culture.

In 2004, the government brought in a law that forbade school students from wearing anything that showed their faith, such as the Jewish skullcap (a small round cap worn by some Jewish men and boys) or the Muslim hijab. This has led to racial tension, particularly between Muslims for whom religion is a vital part of their life and non-Muslims who fear changes in French culture.

In the media

'Our borders have become increasingly porous [easy to get through] from both the Canadian North and Mexico to the South. Illegal aliens [immigrants] are crossing them, virtually unstopped, in the millions every year. These crossings, which have become increasingly violent, are allowing multiple teams of terrorists to enter our country.'

An organization that campaigns against illegal immigration in the USA puts out the message that illegal immigrants from Mexico are criminals.

Roma and Travellers

The Roma and 'Travellers' of Europe are affected by ideas about cultural differences too. They have their own language, customs and lifestyle. They move from place to place, unlike the majority of the population, who are settled. Many settled people hold racist views about them, believing they are lazy and likely to commit crime, or mislead people.

This Roma family lives in poor conditions in eastern Slovakia. As elsewhere in eastern Europe, the Roma suffer from a higher rate of poverty, unemployment, crime and disease than the majority population in Slovakia.

Rejected for being Roma

Somewhere between 150,000 and 300,000 Roma live in the Czech Republic, where racism against them is common. They are poorly educated and it is hard for them to find a job – around 70% are unemployed. A 2004 report described how, the previous year, Mrs Zupková applied for a job in the canteen at Hradec Králové University in Bohemia. She didn't get it. The catering manager told the employment office she refused Mrs Zupková because she was Roma. She thought the Roma people were bad workers and was also worried that her customers would be unhappy if they saw a Roma serving food. In the first case of its kind in the country, the catering company was charged in court for racism.

TALK ABOUT

Look at these stereotypes about different races and kinds of people, and think of some others. Do you agree or disagree with them?

✳ Black people are good at sports.

✳ Jewish people have successful businesses.

✳ Muslims are very religious.

✳ Women are better than men at taking care of babies and children.

For ideas on how to extend discussions, please see the Notes for Teachers on page 47.

Feeling superior

The catering manager in this case thinks that the majority of Czech people are better than the Roma people. Sometimes, people's pride in their country makes them feel superior to minority groups they see as outsiders, or to people from other lands. They claim they are trying to protect their way of life, which they believe is better than any other.

In the USA, for example, about 15% of the population are Hispanic, and more Hispanics arrive each year. Greg Letiecq, leader of an anti-immigration group in Virginia, complained that: *'It's the folks who come in and try to maintain the culture of the country they came from. They don't seem to embrace the American culture, the English language, the social norms of American culture.'* Such feelings can lead to racism against newcomers with a different lifestyle and culture.

This is a Hispanic neighbourhood in Chicago, USA. Hispanic people like to maintain their culture but they like to mix with others too. A 2006 survey showed that one-third of all Hispanic adults and half of Hispanic children spoke English very well.

Chapter 3

What do racists do?

As we have seen, racism can take many forms. It can affect people of all ages. At school, children might not want to work or play with others who have a different skin colour or culture because they think they don't 'fit in' with how everyone else acts and looks. Schoolchildren might behave in this way because they find it easier to stick with people who are like them. This is hurtful and unfair to those who are left out.

Sometimes children call other children names or tease them because of their background, what they look like, the way they talk, the clothes they wear or the food they eat. This is very distressing for the children who are treated in this way. In extreme cases, a group of racist bullies might even beat up a child they've been bullying.

The effects of racism

Racism can have a terrible effect on the individuals who experience it. It can make them feel sad, hurt and extremely lonely. They may become depressed and lose their self-esteem. They might start wishing they were different, or think that somehow they are to blame or could have stopped the racist bullying from happening. Victims of racist bullying might even pretend to be ill so that they don't have to go to school. All these difficulties stop them from focusing on their schoolwork and from making friends. They may start doing badly and getting into trouble with the teachers.

In general, Muslim children in the USA have experienced a rise in racism since the terrorist attacks on the country in September 2001.

Racist abuse can have a terrible effect on young people's lives, both inside and outside school.

Osama al-Najjar is a 15-year-old Arab from Jordan who lives in New York, USA, with his family. Osama shares his first name with Osama Bin Laden, the Islamist who ordered the attacks on New York on 11 September 2001. At school, Osama was constantly jeered at, and endured racist abuse because of his name. People called him 'Bin Laden' and 'terrorist'. He says the teachers were worse than his classmates. His parents complained to the school but nothing was done. Osama began to do badly in his studies, got into fights and ran away from home several times. Osama became so depressed that he tried to kill himself. *'I was just sick. I wasn't thinking straight. I had nothing else to take the pain away,'* he said. After he got better, he changed his name to Sammy in the hope that the abuse would stop. But he is still proud of his Arab background.

FACTS

✳ In 2005, a survey in Hampshire, UK, asked children in years 2, 6, 7 and 9 if they had been picked on because of their skin colour or religion or because they didn't speak English at home. In all four year groups, almost every single pupil from an ethnic minority (a different ethnic group from most people) answered 'yes'.

It happened to me

'I'm the only Asian person in my class and used to get picked on for my colour, but I dealt with it. I feel now though that it's made me racist against white people. I hate myself for it. I just wish people from different races would leave each other alone.'

Shireen, a 15-year-old girl, described her experience, which made her feel bitter and negative.

Mixed heritage families

Racism may not just be an issue at school, it can cause problems within the family too. Children from mixed heritage families may have to put up with racism from one side or even both sides of the family because they are not like either side but a mixture of both. For example, some white people find it hard to accept a black person marrying into the family. On the other hand, there are black people who are proud of their identity and do not welcome a white person joining the family. There is evidence that, over time, people tend to change their attitudes and become more tolerant.

White people suffer too

Racism also affects white people. Mandy in the UK described how it made her angry: *'I get really annoyed that lots of people at my school are racist towards Asians. I'm not Asian, but have friends who are. My family doesn't like Asian people.'* In the USA, white kids who adopt black fashions and music tastes may be bullied for 'acting black'. From this, it is clear that racism can affect lots of people.

A family group of mixed heritage. Britain has one of the fastest-growing mixed heritage populations in the world – despite the difficulties faced by couples from different backgrounds.

Organized racism

When racists get together, they can affect entire communities. Some people join groups to try to influence other people and carry out actions against people of a different skin colour or culture. They may call them names, spray racist messages on walls, or smash the windows of their homes.

Organized racism can make whole communities feel frightened. If there are groups of racists hanging around on the street corners, the idea of even popping out to the shops or to visit friends can become scary. People do not feel safe in their own home if the attackers know where they live. Sometimes, families feel they have no choice but to move away, hoping they will not be faced with racism in their new homes.

Members of a far-right organization in Germany on a demonstration. These neo-Nazis (modern Nazis) take their ideas from Adolf Hitler, who believed in a pure, white German race. This is why they sometimes attack non-white people.

Violence in Germany

Organized racism occurs around the world. It is an increasing problem in eastern Germany, where neo-Nazi groups scapegoat immigrants for economic problems and blame them for the high levels of unemployment. They often target black people. In 2006, a group of neo-Nazi teenagers attacked a 12-year-old Ethiopian boy near the town of Magdeburg. They forced him at gunpoint to lick their boots. The attackers were charged in court. The judge said the only reason for the attack was the colour of the boy's skin.

FACTS

* **The far-right British National Party (BNP) became active in the Barking and Dagenham region of east London from 2001. Its campaign appeared to target members of the growing African communities whom it accused of taking away housing from the local people. The BNP campaign seems to have been the reason for increased racial attacks.**
Source: Unite Against Facism, UK.

Racist attacks, Barking and Dagenham, UK

2002–03	413
2003–04	486
2004–05	693
2005–06	699

Standing for election

Instead of using violence and attacking minority groups, some far-right organizations try to win political support for their views. They put forward candidates for elections and try to persuade people to vote for them. Usually they are not open about their racism because this may put people off. Instead they pose as respectable politicians who want to improve their community. They talk about the difficulties that affect ordinary people, such as poor housing and a lack of decent jobs. Instead of looking to the government to sort out these issues, they scapegoat immigrants and ethnic minorities. Some people, who want to find reasons for the hardships they suffer, may accept this simple argument, which leads to a growth in racism.

This graffiti on a wall in Warsaw, Poland, shows the Nazi swastika. Neo-Nazi groups are illegal in Poland, but they promote their views on the streets and on the Internet.

Race riots

An instance where far-right groups stirred up racism took place in Oldham, a town in northern England. Oldham has high levels of poverty and few job opportunities. Large numbers of Asians live in Oldham, generally in separate areas from white people. Both Asians and white people are affected by the economic problems.

In 2000, the far-right BNP became active in the town. The BNP said that the local government favoured Asians. The BNP encouraged white people to blame Asians for their misfortunes. Tensions rose until they boiled over into violent race riots in 2001. During the riots, up to 500 young Asians fought the police with petrol bombs, bricks and bottles.

A scene during the Oldham riots of 2001, in which cars were set on fire and windows smashed. The riots began when a group of racists attacked the Asian community.

TALK ABOUT

Here are some different ways for teachers to deal with racist bullies at school. Which method do you think would work best, and why? Which methods would not work well?

✳ **Ignoring the incident.**

✳ **Telling the children off and punishing them.**

✳ **Explaining why racism is wrong.**

✳ **Involving everyone in the school in dealing with the issue and trying to reduce racism through the curriculum.**

Uniting against racism

After these terrible events, an organization called Oldham United Against Racism (OUAR) brought people together from local trade unions and voluntary, religious and political groups. They decided to try to improve relations between whites and Asians. The members went around Oldham handing out community newspapers, which explained it was untrue that Asians were being favoured. They talked about the dangerous ideas of the BNP and produced materials to remind people about what happened in the Nazi Holocaust before and during World War II. OUAR held large public meetings to bring people together and break down the barriers between communities. The hard work of anti-racist groups like this ensured that the BNP did badly in Oldham in the 2005 election.

These children in Belgium hold a banner saying, 'Diversity is Reality'. They believe that people should accept others who are different from them and learn to live with one another peacefully.

Chapter 4

Hidden racism

Often individuals aren't deliberately racist, but certain ethnic minorities are still treated unfairly in society. Even though the law may say that everyone should be treated equally, people don't always stick to the rules. They might not mean to be racist, but certain ideas they have make them act that way. This is hidden, or institutional, racism.

At school

Hidden racism can exist in some schools. In the UK, for example, the results of a report in 2007 showed that black pupils were praised less, told off more and punished more harshly than others. Their teachers may not be deliberately racist; they might be acting in this way without thinking. There is a common stereotype which states that black children are no good at schoolwork. Black children might find themselves placed in the lower sets for lessons – especially the boys. These groups generally have poorer resources, so it is hard for the children to do well.

FACTS

Research shows that there is hidden racism in some police forces. Even if individual police officers are not racist, they may accept stereotypes about ethnic communities. For example, in Australia, some believe that the police are more likely to suspect the indigenous Aboriginal population of committing a crime than the white population. The statistics below could show that the police believe the stereotypes and so arrest and convict the indigenous population more readily.

✳ In 2005, in Western and Southern Australia, indigenous people were between 13 and 19 times more likely than non-indigenous people to be in prison.

✳ A 2003 study showed that in New South Wales in 2001, nearly one in five indigenous men appeared in court charged with committing a crime.

At work

Hidden racism also exists in the workplace. African-Americans and Hispanic people in the USA are often treated unfairly. They tend to live in poorer housing and go to worse schools than white people. When they grow up, they usually get lower-paid jobs. Even if they succeed in going to college, there are still barriers to finding a good job.

Most scientists in the USA are white or east Asian men. There are few African-American or Hispanic scientists. Erich Jarvis, a neurobiologist (a scientist who studies the nervous system) in North Carolina, was lucky to receive funding from an organization that helps students from ethnic minorities to go to college. His family was poor. *'We were lower middle class,'* he says. *'I was not like those students who got a car when they graduated. It was the other way around. I had to help my parents.'*

Most of the children in this classroom are black. In the USA, many black children live in poorer areas than white people and attend different schools.

Racism in colleges

Research has shown that, as well as the issue of money, there is a lack of role models for African-Americans and Hispanics to follow, so students from these groups are reluctant to apply to college. There is evidence that some university departments might not even take these students on, because they think they won't fit in. Those who do get a place may indeed feel like outsiders, and might not stay.

Justin Gatlin of the USA runs the 200-metre semi-finals at the Olympic Games in Athens, Greece, in 2004. The stereotype that African-American people are good at sports may be rooted in the fact that poorer people have more opportunity to succeed in sports than in other professions.

TALK ABOUT

Although it is illegal to be openly racist in the media, this does not mean that all people are treated equally. Think about films and TV programmes, and compare the roles played by people of various races and cultures.

* Do you think that different people are provided with equal opportunities in the media?

* Do people of different races all have an equal chance to play powerful and interesting characters? Can you spot any stereotypes?

Hurricane Katrina

Hidden racism goes on all the time in education and in the workplace. For many people, the disaster after Hurricane Katrina hit the New Orleans area in 2005 showed how big an issue hidden racism really is.

After the hurricane, the poorly maintained levees broke. (The levees were walls along the Mississippi River to protect New Orleans from flooding.) Around 80% of New Orleans was flooded. Thousands lost their homes. Most of these people were African-Americans who lived in cheap, low-lying housing. Large numbers were unable to escape New Orleans because they were poor and did not own a car. There were hundreds of tragic deaths. One elderly man managed to drag his wife in her wheelchair to the roof of their home. When the floodwaters rose to the roof, he kept hold of her. Eventually, the flood pulled her away to her death. Help for people trapped in New Orleans was extremely slow to arrive. The rapper Kanye West said on TV that *'[President George W.] Bush doesn't care about black people.'* Many Americans agreed that hidden racism within the US government had been the reason for the slow response.

Amid the floods in New Orleans, anxious people wait on their balconies for rescue boats to come. A man directs the rescuer to the waiting families.

Chapter 5

What is religious prejudice?

Religious prejudice is based on difference, like racism. It usually affects people who look obviously different from the majority or have their own particular customs, such as Jews, Sikhs and Muslims.

Anti-Semitism

One Jewish family was shocked to experience anti-Semitism (hatred of Jews) in the small town of Tampa Bay in Florida, USA. They were called names, had filth put through their letter box and their car was damaged and painted with swastikas – the Nazi symbol. Their 14-year-old daughter was scared to go out to walk the dog. The family were determined to stay in their home though. They explained their story at the town meeting and gained some support from their neighbours, and they put up security cameras to put off the vandals.

Anti-Semitism occurs in other Western countries too. In the UK, for example, there has been a rise in attacks on Jews. Sometimes people attack Jews because they link them to Israel, a Jewish country. A few people who were angry about Israel's war with Lebanon in 2006 went out and attacked Jews because of this anger towards Israel.

Anti-Semitic vandals have drawn swastikas on this synagogue wall in Geneva, Switzerland. Half the people in a 2007 survey in six European countries thought that Jews were more loyal to Israel than their own country. This idea is a common stereotype.

Children say their morning prayers at a Jewish school in the USA.

In the
media

'It was 6pm on a Saturday evening when 12-year-old Jasmine Kranat and her friend boarded the 303 metro-bus in Colindale, north London. The two young girls, who had been to Asda to buy ingredients to make smoothies for a sleepover, were chatting animatedly when nine black and Asian teenagers, who Jasmine had never met before, joined them on the back seat and forced them into the corner.

Three of the teenagers, all 14-year-old girls, began aggressively pestering them. *"Are you Jewish?"* they kept asking. Jasmine, dressed in jeans and from a proudly Jewish, left-wing family, cleverly replied: *"I'm English."* But the dead giveaway, apart from her ringlets of dark brown hair, was that she blushed bright red. Unlike her Christian friend, who wore a crucifix and would be untouched by the marauding [prowling] teenagers, Jasmine was about to receive the beating of her life just because she was born Jewish.'

David Cohen, Evening Standard, 27 September 2006.

Islamophobia

Fear and hatred of Muslims, which has commonly become known as Islamophobia, is on the rise in Western countries. In the USA, for instance, a 2006 poll found that 39% of Americans felt some prejudice against Muslims, and 22% wouldn't want Muslim neighbours. This prejudice has led to a rise in attacks on Muslims, including name-calling, setting mosques on fire, and even murder.

Ideas about Islam

Why has this prejudice come about? It is partly because many people in Western countries think that Islam is a particularly strict religion. They believe that it is old-fashioned and has harsh laws against people who don't obey the rules. They think that Muslim women have no freedom. For example, many Muslim girls and women wear the hijab and dress modestly, covering their arms and legs. They dress in this way according to their religious and cultural customs. But some people in the West think that females are forced by men to adopt the hijab, and they are not free because they cannot dress as they please.

This mosque is in Berlin, Germany. Non-Muslims fear that Muslims are 'taking over' by building their own mosques and businesses, although the proportion of Muslims in Western countries remains small.

These schoolgirls wear the Muslim hijab. There has been a big debate in many European countries over whether Muslim girls should be allowed to wear the hijab to school.

As well as the issue of women's freedom, some non-Muslims think that Islam is a violent religion that calls for terrorist action against non-Muslims. This belief has grown since the Muslim terrorist attacks on the USA of 11 September 2001. Al-Qaeda, the extreme Islamist organization that led the attacks, has threatened a war against Western countries. In response, the USA has led what it calls the 'war on terror' to try to stop Islamic terrorism. Some people in Western countries are afraid of Muslims because they think they might support Al-Qaeda. In fact, the vast majority of Muslims do not have extreme views and are completely peaceful.

It happened to me

Ten-year-old Alana Scott in Jacksonville in Florida, USA, said she was not allowed to perform with her school orchestra because she wore a hijab. 'We were on the school bus on the way to the concert hall. My cello teacher asked, *"Why do you wear that nun thing?"* When I explained, he made rude comments and said I couldn't perform because I wasn't wearing the right uniform. He said, *"Get off the bus or I'll have you and your mother arrested."* I don't understand why he hates me so much. Sometimes teachers don't know everything. It made me feel horrible.'

Religion in schools

As you can see, religious prejudice causes many tensions in society. In Western countries, these tensions have led to a big debate about religion in education. At school, you probably learn about Christianity, the main religion of your country. You also study other faiths and celebrate festivals from different cultures and countries. As one Christian child in the UK says, *'I definitely prefer a mixed school because if it wasn't mixed, it would be boring. I wouldn't be learning about Islam or the Hindu or Sikh religions in RE. It's good fun.'*

Feeling alone

Yet some children feel anxious if there are only a few pupils of their religion at school. They would rather be at a school with others like them. A Sikh child says, *'I want to go to a Sikh school because in this school there are so many Muslims. At Eid most Muslim pupils stay at home and there are only five or six of us left in the class.'* For this reason, some parents prefer their children to attend faith schools, such as Catholic, Jewish or Muslim schools. They want their children to be able to follow their faith freely at school and learn about their religion. However, some people believe this stops children from different religions getting to know one another and can lead to an increase in racism.

Sikh boys study at their temple. Sikhs often suffer racist abuse because they wear a turban. Some ignorant people think they look like Muslim terrorists, who also cover their heads.

Learning about others

Whether or not children of different faiths are educated together, it is everyone's responsibility to get to know people of different religions. If you're from the main religion – or do not have a religion – you can make the effort to meet others from different faiths. If you're from a minority religion, you can become more involved in the society around you so that people understand you better.

These children of different religions perform a Diwali play inside a Hindu temple.

TALK ABOUT

Think about the pros and cons of faith schools. Are these schools a good or a bad thing?

Pros

✳ **You learn about your own faith.**

✳ **You're protected from religious prejudice against your faith.**

✳ **You might grow up more confident.**

✳ **You can follow religious rules at school, for example for diet and clothing, without being teased by others.**

Cons

✳ **You don't get to mix with others from different backgrounds.**

✳ **You may have to travel a long way to school.**

✳ **Children from the majority population will not have a first-hand chance to learn about other religions.**

✳ **Many faith schools are private, so only well-off families can afford to send their children to them.**

Chapter 6

Racism against migrants

People move to other countries for many reasons. They may move to find work, for a better life or to feel safe. Today, a higher number of people live outside their country of birth than ever before in history. Yet migrants still make up only about 3% of the world's population – about 191 million people in 2005.

Migrant movements

The majority of migrants head for More Economically Developed Countries (MEDCs). One out of every four migrants lives in North America, while one in every three lives in Europe. Refugees form a small proportion of the total number of migrants – just 7% in 2005. Most refugees flee from Less Economically Developed Countries (LEDCs) to other nearby LEDCs.

As we saw in Chapter 1, migrants often encounter racism. It is not just to do with skin colour but also because of differences in culture, religion and language. Migrants to Europe from Australia, South Africa and the USA do not generally face the same level of racism if they are white and English-speaking.

This bar chart shows the 20 countries with the highest number of international migrants in 2005.
Source: United Nations Population Fund, 2006.

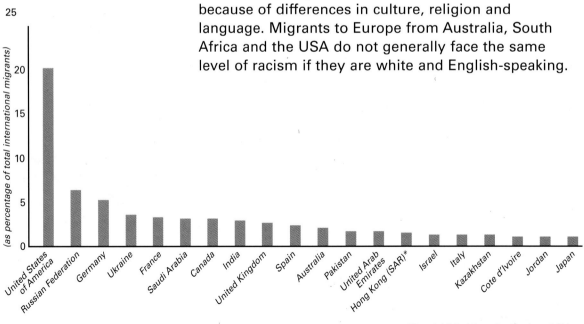

*Special Administrative Region of China

Fears lead to racism

Racism can also arise because some people fear that the newcomers are taking jobs and homes from local people. Usually, migrant workers earn low wages, doing the jobs that locals are not prepared to do. And although it may be true that there is a shortage of decent housing, the situation may be similar in areas without migrants. Local people often don't see the issues this way though. They might also be scared that large numbers of migrants will change the culture of their country. Such fears are often whipped up by some newspapers and other elements in the media. This helps to explain why eastern European migrants to western Europe may face racism even though they are white.

Poland joined the European Union in 2004, giving Polish workers the right to work in other European Union countries. Within two years, around 750,000 Poles had come to the UK to work. Some opened shops, like this one in London.

Poles in Scotland

This has been the case in some parts of Scotland. Between 2004 and 2007, around 40,000 Polish workers came to Scotland. They took on jobs as builders and farm workers, and also as bar staff and doormen in pubs and clubs. Some Scottish people resent the newcomers. At the weekends, some Scottish drinkers hurl racist insults at the Polish workers and occasionally even attack them. In 2007, one Pole, Patryk Mnich, was beaten up in the street in Pilrig in Edinburgh and was left fighting for his life. However, many Scots welcome the Poles, who are bringing new businesses, skills, food and cultural activities to Scotland.

THAT POLISH SHOP
KRAKOWIANKA
020 7403 7425   020 7403 7425

Asylum seekers and refugees

Many people in Western countries are scared that there are not only too many migrants, but too many refugees as well. Only one-fifth of the world's refugees manage to reach Europe or North America. Even though they have fled persecution to move to a safe country, they are not always welcomed.

Claiming asylum

When they first arrive, refugees have to claim asylum – the right to protection in a new country. Known as asylum seekers, they cannot work until their claim is accepted. (If they are refused asylum, they are supposed to return home.) Asylum seekers receive homes, health care and education, even though they are not from the country and do not pay income tax. Many local people feel it is unfair because asylum seekers are getting 'something for nothing.' These economic arguments fuel racist thought and sometimes racist behaviour. Yet most refugees are young and fit, and often well-educated. They are keen to work and contribute to their new country.

In Western countries, some asylum seekers are held in detention centres, like the one shown here. The government decides if they will be given asylum. In Australia, all asylum seekers are placed in detention centres.

Asylum seekers at school

Although their parents are unable to work, the children of asylum seekers can go to school. It is good for them to mix with other children, but there are difficulties too. As well as recovering from the upheaval of fleeing their country, they may be suffering trauma from terrible experiences. As one Scottish teacher explained, *'We always have to remember what some of these children have been through; the children from one family had watched their mother being killed.'* Some children are sympathetic and help the new children, but others – both black and white – may pick on them because they are different and perhaps can't speak the language. Many refugee children encounter racist bullying. If this happens, it is important for the staff and pupils in schools to try to stop it straight away.

The young refugee in the middle has come to the UK from Ethiopia. It was a challenge adapting to school life after living in a refugee camp in Kenya for many years.

DOs & DON'Ts

✳ Do talk about what it means to be a refugee.

✳ Try to find out about the country the refugees come from.

✳ Do put up some signs in the refugees' language and pictures from their country.

✳ Learn some playground and indoor games that don't involve speaking.

✳ Try not to say their name wrong.

✳ Don't ignore refugees at your school. Instead, arrange a buddy for each new pupil.

Hard to settle

Most refugees hope to return home once their country is safe again. For some, this isn't possible. If they come from a country that has been at war for decades, such as Afghanistan, they may need to make a new life in their adopted country. This is not easy. Mahmood came with his family from Afghanistan to seek asylum in Australia when he was 11. They spent three years in a detention centre on Naura, a tiny island in the Pacific, before arriving in Canberra, Australia. He says, *'When you are on the journey, you think that this is going to be the hardest thing about getting to Australia, and that everything is going to be easy afterwards. But once you get here, you realize that this is just the start. Adapting to a new society is like running a hurdle race. No sooner have you jumped over one and you have to jump over another one.'*

A piñata is a brightly coloured paper container filled with sweets and toys. It is a Mexican tradition to play a game to break the piñata while blindfolded and free the sweets and toys. Children play this game at birthday parties.

Many migrants also hope to return home after working for a few years. Some become immigrants and stay in the country. Over time, migrants and refugees gradually settle and integrate (mix with and become accepted) in their new country. The new communities make their own contribution to society.

Positive changes, reducing racism

In the USA, for instance, there has been a huge Mexican influence. Americans regularly eat Tex-Mex food, which is a mixture of northern Mexican and south-western American food. Foods from Mexico such as chocolate, peanuts and coconuts are common, and salsa (a spicy tomato sauce) is now more popular than ketchup on American tables. Americans have adopted Mexican traditions, such as hanging a piñata at birthday parties. Celebrities originally from Mexico include the actress Salma Hayek and world-champion wrestler, Oscar Gutierrez.

Gradually over time, as immigrants adapt to the country and local people get to know them, the tensions and racism are reduced. It has to be a two-way process, requiring effort from people already in the country and newcomers alike.

TALK ABOUT

Find out where the families of all the children in your class come from. Even if they were born in the country, perhaps their parents, grandparents or great-grandparents came from another land.

✱ What have people from each of these countries brought to your country?

✱ Have you been able to experience different cultures, such as food, sport, games or music, because of families from other countries coming to your home?

Chapter 7

What can we do about racism?

Some people face racism directly. They get picked on at
school or in the street. Others feel under attack as a
group. Perhaps they read or hear things that are rude
about them. Some see people acting in a racist way,
even though it is not directed at them.

What if it happens to you?

At first, you may have to cope with it
alone. If someone shouts hurtful things at
you, try to act calmly. Take deep breaths.
Avoid shouting back or starting a fight.
Although it is hard not to get upset or
angry, it's worthwhile trying to remain
calm. If you do not respond, the bullies
may simply become bored and leave you
alone. Then it might be best just to walk
or run away, or if you feel confident you
could tell the bullies to leave you alone.

Remember that racism comes from
ignorance. Don't be tempted to stoop to
the level of the bullies and insult them
back. Try to keep out of their way and
spend time with your friends doing
things that you enjoy. Think positively
about yourself. You can show the bullies
that you are strong and won't be put
down by racism.

*There are many good
websites that can offer
sensible advice on coping
with racism.*

Finding help

Sometimes you may need to get help from others. Talk to your friends, relatives or a teacher you can trust. There are websites and organizations that can offer advice (see page 47). It helps if you know your rights. Racism is against the law, and racists can be punished, even if they are children.

DOs & DON'Ts

Young people have explained how they would like teachers to respond to racism at school:

✳ **Do listen to how we feel.**

✳ **Do let us know that you are not racist and that you will help us.**

✳ **Do take action, however small the problem is.**

✳ **Don't ignore us because you haven't seen the racism yourself. It happens when staff aren't around.**

✳ **Don't jump to conclusions. Investigate the issue carefully before punishing someone.**

✳ **Don't assume that all the teachers understand about different races, cultures and religions. All staff, including supply teachers, should have training.**

Helping your friends

If you see racist bullying going on, don't ignore it. Remember that racism is not just to do with skin colour. Teasing someone for wearing traditional clothes or not speaking your language properly is also racist. If your own classmates are saying hurtful things, you might feel able to talk to the bullies yourself. Otherwise, tell a member of staff you trust. Take action straight away, or the bullying could get worse. If the situation becomes violent, it's best not to get involved in the fight. Get help immediately.

Once things have calmed down, offer your support to the person being bullied. He or she will want to have someone to talk to and to stick up for them. If you and your friends spend time with that person, he or she is less likely to be picked on.

A whole-school issue

The whole school community should tackle racism in school. The pupils who are responsible for racism must understand that what they are doing is wrong, while those affected should be supported. It's important for teachers to talk to the bullies. Some of them may be acting in a racist way to be part of a gang. They are scared that if they don't act like the others, they will be kicked out of the gang or lose face with the other members. Teachers need to understand their fears and encourage them to change their behaviour; it is not enough just to punish them.

It is helpful if all children learn about the different countries their classmates come from, and their culture and customs. It can help to challenge racist ideas.

No one should ever stay silent about racism. It is up to all of us to tackle it.

DOs & DON'Ts

If your friend is suffering from racist bullying, read the action points below to see how you can help.

✳ Do listen to your friend talking about his or her experiences. It is important to be able to express anger and sadness about what is happening.

✳ Do take your friend's concerns seriously and show sympathy. Make it clear that you will help sort out the problem.

✳ If your friend is scared to ask for help, find another person to tell a responsible adult about the bullying.

✳ Don't join in with the racists in the hope that they'll leave you alone if you do.

(Source: ChildLine, UK)

Every year on Holocaust Memorial Day, people around the world remember the Holocaust in which six million Jews died. As part of the ceremony in Jerusalem, Israel, Prime Minister Ehud Olmert lays a wreath.

Making a difference

There are plenty of positive things you can do to help stop racism. Firstly, think before you speak. Be careful about how you talk about people from different cultures. In the USA, some non-Hispanics talk about everyone from South or Central America as 'Mexicans', even though many are not from Mexico. This can be hurtful. Never laugh at a racist joke, just interrupt and say you don't find it funny.

Be open to learning about how different people lead their lives. Look out for multicultural events such as carnivals and join in. Make the effort to get to know people from other cultures. You may be surprised to find how much you have in common, and you will learn a lot too. Find out how people from different countries and cultures have benefited your country. You'll probably find that many of your favourite sportspeople, musicians and film stars come from different places.

TALK ABOUT

Imagine moving to another country with your family under difficult circumstances. Your language, culture and religion are different from everyone else's. Think about some of the difficulties you would face. Which of these issues would you find the hardest to cope with?

* Learning a new language.

* Making new friends.

* Dealing with racist bullying.

* Not being able to practise your religion at school.

* Eating different foods.

* Missing your wider family and friends.

* Missing your home town.

Understanding the media

Don't believe everything you read or see. Learn to think carefully about what you see in the media. Try to work out if programmes or articles in newspapers or magazines are being fair to different groups, or if they include stereotypes.

Anti-racist activities

Anti-racist organizations hold public events to oppose racism and promote understanding. For example, on Holocaust Memorial Day, people gather to remember the racism and anti-Semitism of the Nazis that led to the deaths of six million Jews. They talk about how to stop racism today. You might like to join a group that brings people from different backgrounds together, such as a sports team or theatre group. You'll enjoy an exciting activity while doing your bit to break down barriers between people and reduce racism in society.

At the Notting Hill Carnival in London, people from different backgrounds enjoy a colourful parade, lively music, dancing and delicious food.

Glossary

African-American A term to describe Americans whose families originally came from Africa, usually as slaves.

Al-Qaeda An Islamic terrorist organization that wants American forces to leave the Middle East. Al-Qaeda also wants to set up Islamic governments across the Muslim world.

candidate In an election, a person who tries to get people to vote for him or her so he or she can join the local council or become a Member of Parliament.

colony A country that is ruled over by another country.

detention centre A place like a prison, where asylum seekers may be sent until the government decides if they are allowed to stay in the country as refugees.

ethnic group A group of people who share a culture, tradition, way of life and sometimes language. An ethnic minority is a group of people who have a different culture, religion, skin colour or language from most other people in their society.

far-right organizations Groups who tend to be conservative in their outlook and to believe their country is better than others. They often have racist views towards people from ethnic minorities and migrants.

hidden racism When individuals are not deliberately racist, but the way things work in society means that people from ethnic minorities are treated unfairly.

Hispanic A person from a Latin-American country.

Holocaust The mass murder of Jewish people, Roma and other groups by the Nazis.

immigrant A person who moves from their home to settle in another country.

indigenous people The people who belong to a particular place.

Less Economically Developed Countries (LEDCs) The poorer countries of the world, including the countries of Africa, Asia (except for Japan), Latin America and the Caribbean.

More Economically Developed Countries (MEDCs) The richer countries of the world, including Europe and northern America.

persecution Treating people badly, often because of their race, religion, culture or beliefs.

poll Asking a number of different kinds of people their opinion on an issue in order to work out what the general view is.

race In daily life, the word 'race' is used to describe a group of people who share certain features, such as black skin.

refugee A person who escapes to another country to seek safety from war, natural disaster or bad treatment.

scapegoating Unfairly blaming a group of people for a problem in society.

slaves People owned by others and forced to work for them for no money.

terrorist A person who uses violent actions to achieve political aims.

trade union An organization of workers that helps protect their working conditions and pay.

welfare system The system in many countries that provides money, housing and services to people who are very poor.

Further information

Notes for Teachers:

The Talk About panels are to be used to encourage debate and avoid the polarization of views. One way of doing this is to use 'continuum lines'. Think of a range of statements or opinions about the topics that can then be considered by the pupils. An imaginary line is constructed that pupils can stand along to show what they feel in response to each statement (please see picture above). If they strongly agree or disagree with the viewpoint they can stand by the relevant sign, if the response is somewhere in between, they stand along the line in the relevant place. If the response is 'neither agree, nor disagree' or they 'don't know' then they stand at an equal distance from each sign, in the middle. Alternatively, continuum lines can be drawn out on paper and pupils can mark a cross on the line to reflect their views.

Books to read

21st Century Debates: Racism by Cath Senker (Wayland, 2003)

Choices and Decisions: Dealing With Racism by Pete Saunders and Steve Myers (Franklin Watts, 2007)

Get Wise: Racism and Prejudice – Why is it Wrong? by Jane Bingham (Heinemann Library, 2005)

What's That Got to Do With Me? Racism by Antony Lishak (Franklin Watts, 2005)

Websites and helplines

Amnesty International USA

The kids' section of AI, which takes action for human rights around the world.
Website:
http://www.amnestyusa.org/Indiv
iduals_at_Risk/AI_Kids/page.do?i
d=1101360&n1=3&n2=34&n3=67

Britkid

A site for young people about race and racism.
Website: http://www.britkid.org/

CBBC Newsround

CBBC pages about racism and what to do about it.
Website:
http://news.bbc.co.uk/cbbcnews/
hi/newsid_1700000/newsid_1703
900/1703902.stm

ChildLine

A free advice and information helpline for young people.
Website:
http://www.childline.org.uk
Phone: 00 44 (0)800 1111

Kidlink

The No More Racism pages from the Kidlink site, which helps children to understand themselves and build links with children from different cultures and countries.
Website:
http://www.kidlink.org/english/v
oice/racism/index.html

Kidscape

A charity that aims to prevent bullying.
Website:
http://www.kidscape.org.uk

NSPCC

Free helpline, open 7 days a week, 24 hours a day.
Website:
http://www.nspcc.org.uk
Phone: 00 44 (0)808 800 5000

Racism No Way!

Australian website with comics, puzzles and quizzes on anti-racist themes for children of 10 and over.
Website:
http://racismnoway.com.au/gam
esroom/

Show Racism the Red Card

A national campaign to stop racism in football.
Website: www.srtrc.org/

Teachernet

This site for teachers has a section with stories and messages from young people.
Website:
http://www.teachernet.gov.uk/w
holeschool/behaviour/tacklingbu
llying/racistbullying/introduction
/storiesandmessages/

Index

Entries in **bold** are for pictures.

African-American people 5,
 25, **25**, 26, 27
Al-Qaeda 31
anti-racism 23, **23**, 45
anti-Semitism 28-9, 45
Asian people 5, 18, 19, 22-3
asylum seekers 36-7, **36**

British National Party (BNP)
 21, 22-3
bullying 5, 16, 22, 37, 42, 43

colonies 6, 7, 7

ethnic groups 5, 17, 21, 24,
 25

faith schools 32-3

gangs 10, 11, 20, 22, 42

Hispanic people 5, **13**, 15,
 15, 25, 26, 39
Holocaust, the 23, 44, **44**, 45

immigrants 7, 12, 13, 20, 21,
 39
indigenous people 24
Islam 10, **10-11**, **12**, 13, **16**,
 28, 30-31, **30-31**
Islamophobia 30
Israel 9, 28, **44**

Judaism 13, 28-9, **29**

laws 7

migrants 8, **8-9**, 12, **34**, 34,
 35, 39
mixed heritage families
 18-19, 19

neo-Nazis 11, 12, 20, **20**, 21

prejudice 4-9, 10, 28, 30, 32

race riots 22, **22**
racism 6-9, 14, 19, 20, 24,
 34-5
 at work 25
 in Australia 11, 24
 in education 24, 26
 in England 22, **22**, 28-9
 in Germany 20, **20**
 in India 5, **5**
 in politics 21
 in Russia 11
 in schools 16-17, 37, 41, 42
 in Scotland 35
 in South Africa 5
 in the USA 27
 preventing 40-45
 victims of 16
racists 10, 20, 22
refugees 8, 34, 36, 37, **37**,
 38, 39
Roma people 6, 14, **14**, 15

scapegoating 12, 20, 21
Sikhism 28, **32**
slavery 6
stereotypes 10-11, 15, 24, 45
 in the media 10, 26, 35, 45

terrorism 10, 12, 17, 31

48

TALK ABOUT

Contents of titles in the series:

Bullying

978 0 7502 4617 0
1. Let's talk about bullying
2. What is bullying?
3. How does it feel to be bullied?
4. Who gets bullied?
5. Why do people bully?
6. Beating bullying
7. Bullying in society

Eating Disorders and Body Image

978 0 7502 4936 2
1. What are eating disorders?
2. Food and the body
3. What does it mean to have an eating disorder?
4. Who gets eating disorders?
5. What causes eating disorders?
6. Preventing problems
7. The treatment of eating disorders

Racism

978 0 7502 4935 5
1. What is racism?
2. Why are people racist?
3. What do racists do?
4. Hidden racism
5. What is religious prejudice?
6. Racism against migrants
7. Nazi racial policies
8. What can we do about racism?

Drugs

978 0 7502 4937 9
1. What are drugs?
2. Why do we take drugs?
3. What about drinking and smoking?
4. What's the law on drugs?
5. What about cannabis?
6. What other drugs are there?
7. Paying the price
8. It's your choice

Homelessness

978 0 7502 4934 8
1. What is homelessness?
2. Why do people become homeless?
3. Homelessness and children
4. Addiction and homelessness
5. Staying clean and healthy
6. Mental health
7. Working and earning
8. Helping the homeless

Youth Crime

978 0 7502 4938 6
1. What is crime?
2. Crime past and present
3. Why does youth crime happen?
4. Behaving badly
5. Crimes of theft
6. Crimes of violence
7. What happens if you commit a crime?
8. What can you do about crime?

WAYLAND